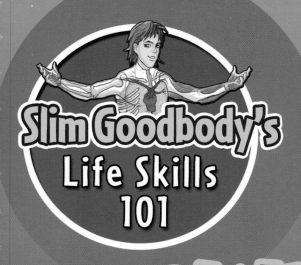

Slim Goodbody's Life Skills 101

WHY ARE YOU PICKING ON ME?

Dealing with Bullies

CRABTREE
Publishing Company
www.crabtreebooks.com

Crabtree Publishing Company
www.crabtreebooks.com

Series Development, Writing, and Packaging:
John Burstein, Slim Goodbody Corp.

Editors:
Reagan Miller, Valerie Weber, and Mark Sachner,
Water Buffalo Books

Editorial director:
Kathy Middleton

Production coordinator:
Kenneth Wright

Prepress technicians:
Margaret Amy Salter, Kenneth Wright

Designer: Tammy West, Westgraphix LLC.

Photos: Chris Pinchback, Pinchback Photography

"Slim Goodbody" and Pinchback photos, copyright,
© Slim Goodbody

"Slim Goodbody" and "Slim Goodbody's Life
Skills 101" are registered trademarks of the Slim
Goodbody Corp.

Photo credits:
iStockPhotos: p. 5 (bottom), 8 (bottom), 13 (right),
  17 (bottom), 19 (top), 20 (middle), 26
Shutterstock: p. 6, 9 (all), 11 (top), 14 (top), 16,
  19 (middle)
© Slim Goodbody: p. 1, 4, 5 (top), 7 (all), 8 (top,
  middle), 11, (bottom), 12, 13 (left), 14 (bottom),
  15, 17 (top), 18 (all), 19 (bottom), 20 (top, bottom),
  21 (all), 22, 23 (all), 24 (all), 25, 27 (all), 28 (all),
  29 (all)

Acknowledgements:
The author would like to thank the following
children for all their help in this project: Stephanie
Bartlett , Sarah Booth, Christine Burstein, Lucas
Burstein, Olivia Davis, Eleni Fernald, Kylie Fong,
Tristan Fong, Colby Hill, Carrie Laurita, Ginny
Lauria, Henry Laurita, Louis Laurita, Nathan
Levig, Havana Lyman, Renaissance Lyman,
Andrew McBride, Lulu McClure, Yanmei
McElhaney, Amanda Mirabile, Esme Power, Emily
Pratt, Andrew Smith, Dylan Smith, Mary Wells

Library and Archives Canada Cataloguing in Publication

Burstein, John
　　Why are you picking on me? : dealing with bullies / John Burstein.

(Slim Goodbody's life skills 101)
Includes index.
ISBN 978-0-7787-4792-5 (bound).--ISBN 978-0-7787-4808-3 (pbk.)

　　1. Bullying--Juvenile literature. I. Title. II. Title: Dealing with bullies.
III. Series: Burstein, John. Slim Goodbody's life skills 101

BF637.B85B87 2010　　　j302.3　　　C2009-903379-8

Library of Congress Cataloging-in-Publication Data

Burstein, John.
　　Why are you picking on me? : Dealing with bullies / John Burstein.
　　　p. cm. -- (Slim Goodbody's life skills 101)
　　Includes index.
　　ISBN 978-0-7787-4808-3 (pbk. : alk. paper) -- ISBN 978-0-7787-4792-5 (reinforced
library binding : alk. paper)
　　1. Bullying--Juvenile literature. I. Title.
BF637.B85B87 2010
302.3--dc22

2009022427

Crabtree Publishing Company

Published in Canada
Crabtree Publishing
616 Welland Ave.
St. Catharines, Ontario
L2M 5V6

Published in the United States
Crabtree Publishing
PMB16A
350 Fifth Ave., Suite 3308
New York, NY 10118

Published in the United Kingdom
Crabtree Publishing
White Cross Mills
High Town, Lancaster
LA1 4XS

Published in Australia
Crabtree Publishing
386 Mt. Alexander Rd.
Ascot Vale (Melbourne)
VIC 3032

CONTENTS

Words in **bold** are defined
in the glossary on page 30.

A TRUE STORY

Kristina and her family had moved to town right before the school year started. Three lonely weeks had passed, but finally Kristina was feeling happier. Her teachers seemed to like her, and she had made a friend named Angela. The two of them had just finished going through the lunch line in the cafeteria when Shelby walked up to them. She bumped into Kristina on purpose.

"Hey, why did you do that?" asked Kristina.

"Cause I felt like it, loser," Shelby replied with a nasty grin.

"Watch it," Angela whispered. "She's really mean."

"I heard that," said Shelby. "Maybe I need something to sweeten me up." With that, Shelby grabbed the dessert off Kristina's tray.

"This should do the trick," Shelby said as she started to walk away.

"That's mine," Kristina told her. "Give it back."

Shelby whirled around. The dessert was in one hand. Her other hand was clenched in a fist.

"If you want something to put in your mouth, how about this?"

Kristina didn't know what to do. Shelby looked much tougher than Kristina. Maybe she should just let her take the dessert. Besides, was a piece of cake worth a fight? But if she let Shelby get away with it, would it happen again?

Hi. My name is Slim Goodbody.

I wrote this book to help you deal with bullies. Bullies are a big problem in schools all around the world.

About one out of every five school children gets bullied.

So if you're being bullied, you're not alone. Millions of other kids have to deal with bullies as well.

Read on to learn some **strategies** to help put an end to bullying.

WHO IS A BULLY?

A bully is someone who picks on somebody else again and again. Bullies like to hurt and frighten kids who they think are weaker or smaller than they are. The person a bully picks on is sometimes called the victim or target. Bullies want to make their victims feel hurt, sad, scared, or hopeless. Many bullies want their victims to cry or react in some way.

bully

victim

Not a Bully

If you tease a friend every once in a while, that does not make you a bully. If your friends play a trick on you, that does not make them bullies. Even if your friend gets into a fight one day, that does not make him or her bully.

Bullies come in all sizes and ages. Some are big and **muscular**. Some are short and skinny. Some bullies are old, and some are young. Some bullies are girls, and some are boys.

Where Does Bullying Happen?

- In classrooms and hallways • In bathrooms, lunchrooms, and locker rooms • On school buses • In parks and on playgrounds • In stores and malls • On the computer and phone

Right and Wrong

If bullying happens so often, does that make it OK? No, it does not! Just because something happens all the time does not make it right. Human beings should be kind to each other. Making other people suffer is just plain wrong. You should treat others as you want others to treat you.

BULLY BASICS

Bullies attack their victims in different ways. Sometimes the attack is **physical**. Physical bullying includes these actions:

- hitting or kicking someone

- bumping or shoving someone

- **threatening** to hurt someone

- pulling someone's hair

- stealing someone's money, books, food, or other things

- hiding or ruining someone's belongings

- forcing someone to do things he or she doesn't want to do

Sometimes the attack is verbal.

Verbal bullying includes these things:

- calling someone bad names
- making fun of someone's family
- teasing or insulting
- telling someone that he or she can't join in a game or group activity
- whispering about and laughing at someone
- making rude noises as someone walks by
- spreading lies and rumors to other kids at school
- spreading lies and rumors about someone on the Internet
- telling someone that he or she can't sit at a lunchroom table

Sometimes the attack is silent.

Silent bullying includes these things:

- refusing to talk with someone
- getting friends to ignore someone
- not including someone in a game or activity
- turning your back on someone and pretending he or she isn't there
- giving someone dirty looks

HOW COME?

You may be wondering why someone would want to hurt someone else. Here is one major reason. People bully others to make themselves feel better!

When bullies make someone else feel upset or afraid, they feel a sense of power over their victims. Power makes bullies feel as if they are better than their victims. It makes them feel better about themselves.

Bullies do not really feel strong inside, though. If bullies felt strong, they would not try to feel powerful by hurting others.

People become bullies for many reasons.

- Bullies may struggle with schoolwork. Bullies can lose confidence in themselves around kids who are doing well in class. They get angry and want to make these kids feel badly about themselves.

- Bullies may struggle to make friends. They may be lonely and use bullying as a way to get attention from other kids.

- Bullies may be popular and do well in school, but they can still be angry inside. Their anger makes them want to hurt others.

- Bullies may not feel that they are getting enough attention from their parents or teachers. Bullying is a way to get noticed.

- Bullies may have learned by example. They may have seen their family members bullying each other. They may have been bullied themselves by brothers or sisters.

- Bullies may be spoiled kids who never learned that they can't always have their way. Bullying gets others to do what they want.

- Bullies may be upset and angry because family members are fighting at home. Instead of talking about their feelings, they attack others.

- Bullies may attack others to try to fit in with a group of friends. If their friends are bullies, they may feel pressure to be a bully too.

11

GOING "FISHING"

You may think that bullies somehow "just know" which kids to bully. That is not true, however. Many bullies start the school year fishing for victims. They keep picking on different kids, hoping to find a perfect target. Bullies keep doing this until someone shows fear, anger, or some sign of weakness. Then bullies know they have "hooked" a victim. Once a bully picks someone to threaten, other bullies may start bullying that kid, too.

Who is a victim?

Victims often have a lot in common.

- They do not feel good about themselves. This is called low **self-esteem**.

- They are shy and don't feel comfortable around others.

- They don't make friends easily and are often alone.

- They're new to the school.

- They cry or become upset easily.

- They hang their heads down and don't look people in the eyes.

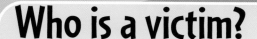

- They cannot **defend** or stand up for themselves.

- They belong to some type of **minority**. For example, Chinese-American kids attending a school with mostly non-Asian students would be in a minority. So would girls playing on a boys' football team.

- They have something that makes them seem different. That difference might be a **disability** that makes them walk or talk with difficulty.

- They are smaller or bigger than most other kids their age.

11:?? Wrong Place, Wrong Time

Sometimes there is no reason why a person gets bullied! Maybe the bully ran out of people to pick on. Maybe someone was in the wrong place at the wrong time when the bully was feeling mean. Some kids get bullied because of something that happened by accident. For example, they tripped and dropped their tray in front of everyone in the lunchroom. Bullies may start teasing them and saying they are clumsy.

LET SOMEONE KNOW

Bullies often tell their victims to keep quiet about the bullying. Don't listen to them! No one has the right to threaten or hurt you. If you are being bullied, the most important thing to do is to tell a friendly, caring adult about what is going on.

You can speak with your mom, dad, grandparents, school principal, or teacher. Most adults know how bullying feels and will want to help you. Together, you can make a plan to get the bullying to stop.

Who, What, Where, and When

When you tell an adult about the bullying, give that person details. Explain:

who the bully is,

what the bully says and does,

where the bullying takes place (in class, on the bus, in the hallway, in the lunchroom), and

when the bullying usually happens (during recess, before school, after class).

Talk about all your feelings. Make it clear to the adult that you are very upset and say, "I need your help."

Do not plan **revenge** against the bully. You could end up in a fight and get hurt. You might get into trouble for fighting. Plus, you don't want to act like a bully yourself!

Bring a Friend

If you don't want to talk to someone alone, bring a friend, **sibling**, or parent. It especially helps to bring someone who has seen the bullying. That person can also talk about what has happened to you.

Write It Out

If you feel too afraid or embarrassed to talk about being bullied, write a letter about it. Give the letter to an adult you trust. Once the adult knows there is a problem, he or she will help you figure out a solution.

BE PREPARED

Telling an adult about the bully is a very important step. There are other things you can do, however, to keep yourself safer:

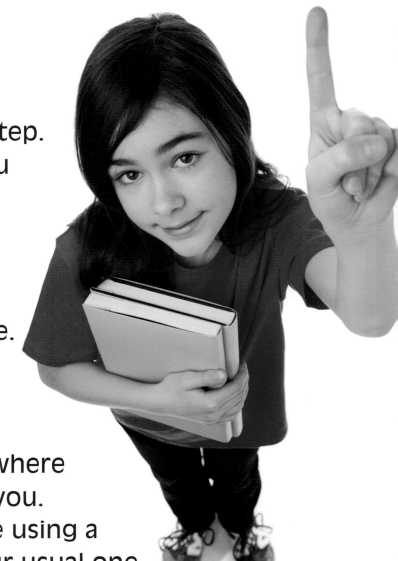

- Avoid places where you have been bullied before.
- Don't travel alone. Walk with a friend or two whenever you can.
- Keep away from places where no one can see or hear you.
- Travel to and from home using a different route than your usual one.
- Leave a little earlier or later for school to avoid meeting the bully.
- Sit near the bus driver on the school bus.
- Walk with a teacher to classes.
- Don't bring fancy things to school.
- Label your belongings in case they get stolen.
- Don't bring any money to school unless you need to.
- Make sure you're not alone in the locker room or bathroom.

LOOK OUT

Ask your teacher to keep a special lookout for any bullying in the halls or on the playground. If your teacher is aware of the problem, he or she can step in at the first sign of trouble. If the bully is in your class, ask your teacher not to partner you two up.

KEEP FRIENDS CLOSE

When friends are around, you will have a better chance to avoid being picked on. Bullies are cowards. They will probably not want to face a whole group of kids at the same time. Here are some ways your friends can help:

- Friends can sit with you in the lunchroom.

- Friends can walk with you in the hallways.

- Friends can stay near you on the playground.

- Friends can walk with you to and from school.

STANDING TALL

Even with friends around, you may still get picked on. Being bullied is not something you should be ashamed of. It is not your fault, but you can help stop it from happening. You can work to change your **body language**.

body drooping

sad face

happy face

gaze straight ahead

shoulders hunched

shoulders back

body straight

gaze down

A bully is more likely to pick on someone who does not look **self-confident**.

Strong and Proud

Think about your favorite movie stars or athletes. Imagine how they would stand and walk if they won an award.

Now try standing and walking as if you have won an award. As you walk along, say to yourself, "I am confident and proud to be me!"

Practice in front of a mirror until you feel comfortable. Ask your parents to watch and give you tips. Soon, these movements will become natural to you. You won't have to think about your body language.

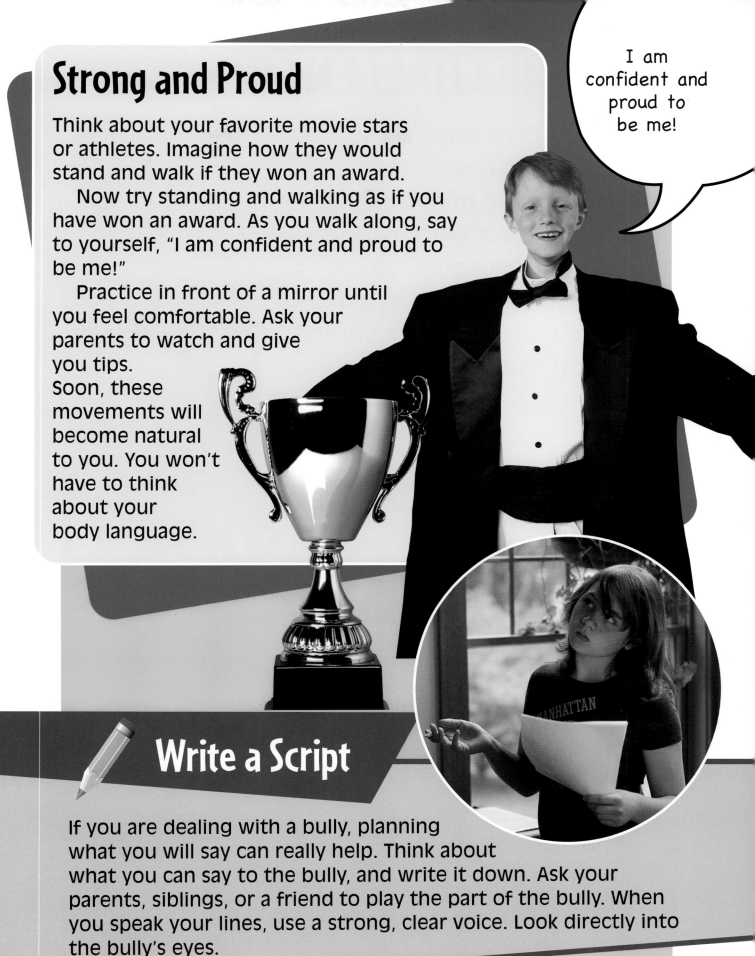

I am confident and proud to be me!

Write a Script

If you are dealing with a bully, planning what you will say can really help. Think about what you can say to the bully, and write it down. Ask your parents, siblings, or a friend to play the part of the bully. When you speak your lines, use a strong, clear voice. Look directly into the bully's eyes.

FACE THE CHALLENGE

So you've talked with an adult and done your best to avoid bullies. The time may still come when you have to face one. There is no one right way to deal with a bully. Each situation is different, but here are some things you can do.

Take a Breath

Take a breath and stand tall.
This will give you self-confidence.

Ear Buds

If you are being teased and called names try playing "Ear Buds." Imagine that you are wearing a special pair of ear buds that do not allow sound in. You can see the bully's lips moving — but not hear what he or she is saying. Or pretend the bully is from outer space and speaking an **alien** language. Imagine the words sound like nonsense.

Ignore the Bore

Ignore the bully. Try to not look at him. Pretend you cannot hear what he is saying. Walk right past him if you can. He is not worth your time.

Keep Your Feelings Inside

If you can't ignore the bully, don't show how upset you are. Don't cry or act angry. Even if you are very upset, don't let it show. If the bully teases you, try to act as if it does not bother you. Bullies are looking for a **reaction**. If they don't get one, it is no longer fun for them to bully and they may walk away.

ANSWERING BACK

If you have to speak back to the bully, remember the statements you have practiced. When you speak, make sure you look the bully in the eyes. Use your strong voice. Don't shout, but speak clearly, calmly, and with confidence.

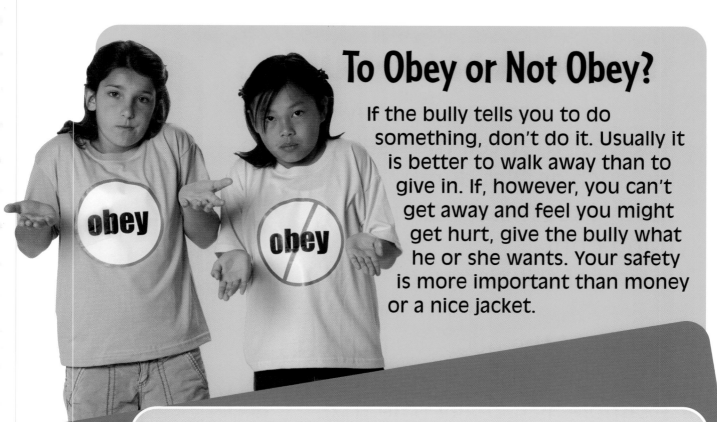

To Obey or Not Obey?

If the bully tells you to do something, don't do it. Usually it is better to walk away than to give in. If, however, you can't get away and feel you might get hurt, give the bully what he or she wants. Your safety is more important than money or a nice jacket.

Make a Joke

If you can get the bully to laugh, he or she might stop being angry and leave you alone. Try turning an insult into a joke. For example, suppose the bully says, "Stupid outfit!" You can say, "Thanks! I'm glad you noticed."

When in Doubt, Shout!

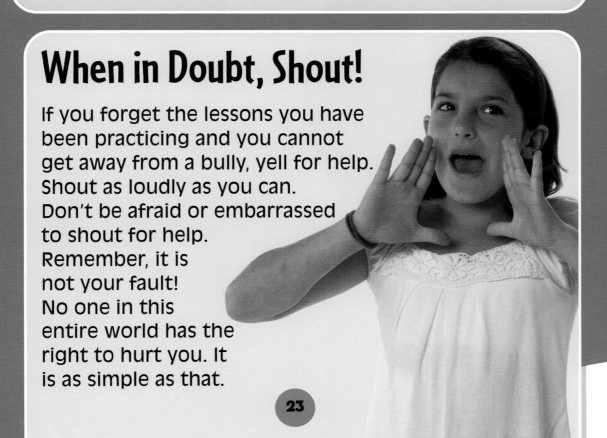

If you forget the lessons you have been practicing and you cannot get away from a bully, yell for help. Shout as loudly as you can. Don't be afraid or embarrassed to shout for help. Remember, it is not your fault! No one in this entire world has the right to hurt you. It is as simple as that.

ARE YOU A SELF-BULLY?

Many victims start out by bullying themselves! They tell themselves mean things, such as "I'm dumb." "Nobody likes me." "I can't do anything right."

This kind of talk destroys your self-confidence. Not only that, most of the negative things you tell yourself are not true! For example, is it really true that NOBODY likes you? Is it really true that you never do ANYTHING right? Of course not!

- I am kind to others.

- I am smart in social studies.

- I have a nice smile.

- I am a fast runner.

To help change this self-bullying, make a list of your positive **traits**. Tape your list to the bathroom mirror or on your bedroom door. Read it to yourself as you brush your teeth each morning. Remind yourself that you are a great person. You deserve respect from others.

Do You Bully Others?

Some kids are bullies without even knowing it! To find out if you are a bully, ask yourself these questions:

- Does it make me feel better to hurt other people? Do I like to call people names or tease others until they cry?

- Do I like to pick on people or take their things?

- Do I push people around to get my way?

- Do I ignore how other people feel if I say or do hurtful things to them?

- Do I embarrass others so people will think I'm cool?

Take Action!

If you decide you are a bully, here are a few things you can do to change:

- Apologize to people you have bullied.

- If you have stolen any money or people's things, return them.

- Be friendly to people you have bullied.

- If you feel as if you're having trouble controlling your feelings, talk to a trusted adult.

Bullying can become a habit. The longer it goes on, the harder it is to stop. Many bullies grow up into adults who bully their families and friends. Now is the time to stop!

HELPING OUT

Bullying usually happens when other kids are around. Bullies want to show off in front of an audience. They want other people to see that they have power over their victims.

If you see someone being bullied, you should speak up. Speaking up can be scary, but it is important to try. Doing nothing is like saying, "Bullying is alright with me." If just one person watching a bullying situation says "Stop it!" half the time the bullying will stop!

Here are some ways you can tell a bully to quit it. You can say:

"That's not funny!"

"I will tell someone if you don't stop."

"How would you like it if someone bullied you?"

"That's not cool."

"Is this your idea of fun? Can't you find something better to do with your time?"

"Do you really want to be so mean? I thought you were better than that."

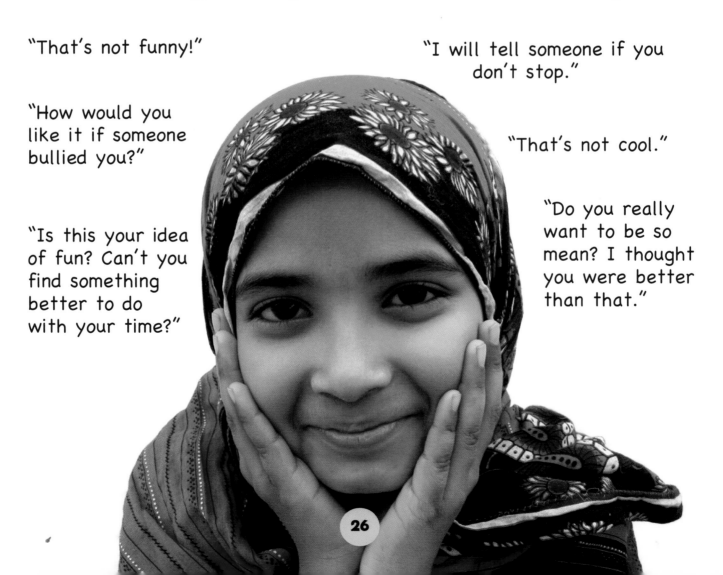

Speaking Up

It is possible that by speaking up, you will turn the bully against you. Be prepared for this, and stand up for yourself. Or exactly the opposite might happen. People may get the idea that you are someone who can't be bullied by others. In addition, the person you help may do the same for you in the future.

Being a Friend

If you see people being bullied, make sure the victims tell their parents or a teacher. Offer to go with them if it will help. If they will not talk to anybody, offer to talk to someone for them.

Get Help

If you feel too scared or upset to speak up, walk away quickly and tell the nearest adult. Get him or her to come and deal with the bully.

BULLY-FREE ZONE

Kids all over the country are starting anti-bullying programs at their schools. You can, too, with a little help from your parents and teachers. Here are some steps you can take:

- Ask your teacher or principal if they will hold an assembly to talk about the problem of bullying.

- Ask your parents to talk about bullying at their PTA or PTO meetings.

- Make a "bully box." People can slip notes about school bullies into the box. The principal and teachers can then talk to the bullies and help them change their **behavior**.

Write a Bill of Rights

Gather your classmates together, and write up a **Bill of Rights** for your school. A Bill of Rights tells what rights all people should have.

Bill of Rights

ALL KIDS

- HAVE THE RIGHT TO FEEL SAFE AND PROTECTED AT SCHOOL

- HAVE THE RIGHT TO FEEL GOOD ABOUT THEMSELVES

- HAVE A RIGHT TO HAVE FUN AT SCHOOL, PARKS, AND PLAYGROUNDS

- HAVE THE RIGHT TO KEEP THEIR PROPERTY

- HAVE THE RIGHT TO BE TREATED FAIRLY

Now You Know

Dealing with bullies is not easy or fun, but dealing with bullies is very important. Now you know what steps to take. Remember, everyone deserves to be treated with respect.

GLOSSARY

alien Not understandable; from another country or outer space

behavior The way a person acts

Bill of Rights A list of privileges that everyone should have. In the United States, the Bill of Rights says that people have the right to choose their own religion, to talk about anything they want, and to gather whenever they want. There are other rights as well.

body language The way a person moves or holds himself or herself that communicates something to other people

defend To protect

disability A physical or mental characteristic that makes it harder for a person to do an activity

gaze A long, steady look

minority A group of people that is thought of as different from the larger group of people. People can be considered minorities because of their race, their gender, or their religion

muscular Having strong muscles

physical Having to do with the body

reaction A response

revenge To harm or punish someone to get back for something done

self-confident Having trust or faith in yourself and in your powers and abilities

self-esteem Respect for yourself as a person

sibling A brother or sister

strategies Plans for achieving goals

threatening Saying that something will be done to hurt someone

traits Qualities or characteristics of someone or something

verbal Expressed using words

BOOKS

Romain, Trevor. *Bullies Are a Pain in the Brain*. Free Spirit Publishing.

Cohen-Posey, Kate. *How to Handle Bullies, Teasers and Other Meanies: A Book That Takes the Nuisance Out of Name Calling and Other Nonsense*. Rainbow Books

Ludwig, Trudy. *Just Kidding*. Adam Gustavson (Illustrator). Tricycle Press

Cooper, Scott. *Speak Up And Get Along!: Learn The Mighty Might, Thought Chop, And More Tools To Make Friends, Stop Teasing, And Feel Good About Yourself*. Joe Fournier (Illustrator). Free Spirit Press

WEB SITES

Kidshealth
kidshealth.org/kid/feeling/emotion/bullies.html
Check out this Web site for information on how bullies operate and what you can do to take care of yourself.

PBS Kids
pbskids.org/itsmylife/friends/bullies/
On this wonderful Web site you can play games, answer questions, find out what other kids think, and watch videos about dealing with bullies.

Kids Against Bullying
pacerkidsagainstbullying.org/
A fun Web site where you can play games, enter contests, find out what other kids are thinking, and vote on bullying issues.

Slim Goodbody
slimgoodbody.com
Discover loads of fun and free downloads for kids, teachers, and parents.

INDEX

About the Author
John Burstein (also known as Slim Goodbody) has been entertaining and educating children for over thirty years. His programs have been broadcast on CBS, PBS, Nickelodeon, USA, and Discovery. He has won numerous awards including the Parent's Choice Award and the President's Council's Fitness Leader Award. Currently, Mr. Burstein tours the country with his multimedia live show "Bodyology." For more information, please visit **slimgoodbody.com**.

Printed in the U.S.A.— CG